FIND OUT ABOUT
Metal

This edition 2002

© Franklin Watts 1994

Franklin Watts
96 Leonard Street
LONDON EC2A 4XD

Franklin Watts Australia
45-51 Huntley Street
Alexandria
NSW 2015

ISBN: 0 7496 4776 0

Dewey Decimal Classification 669

A CIP catalogue record for this book
is available from the British Library

Editor: Annabel Martin
Design: Thumb Design

Photographs: Chris Fairclough Colour Library
15, 19, 20, 21, 22, 23, 25, 26; © Crown Copyright
by kind permission of the Controller of Her
Majesty's Stationery Office 12; Eye Ubiquitous 18,
© Helen Lisher 6, © Dave Fobister 24;
Robert Harding Picture Library 4, 13, 14, 16, 31
© Didier Barrault 30; The Hutchison Library 7;
© Edward Parker 5, © Michael MacIntyre 11;
NASA/Science Photo Library 28, 29; Sheridan
Photo Library © B. Norman 10; ZEFA 8, 9, 17, 27.

Printed in Hong Kong, China

FIND OUT ABOUT
Metal

Henry Pluckrose

W
FRANKLIN WATTS
LONDON•SYDNEY

Iron is a metal.
This famous bridge
was built many years ago.
It was the first bridge
ever to be built of iron.

The blacksmith
works with iron.
He makes shoes for horses.

Iron is found in special rocks.
These contain iron ore.
This rock is dug from the ground.

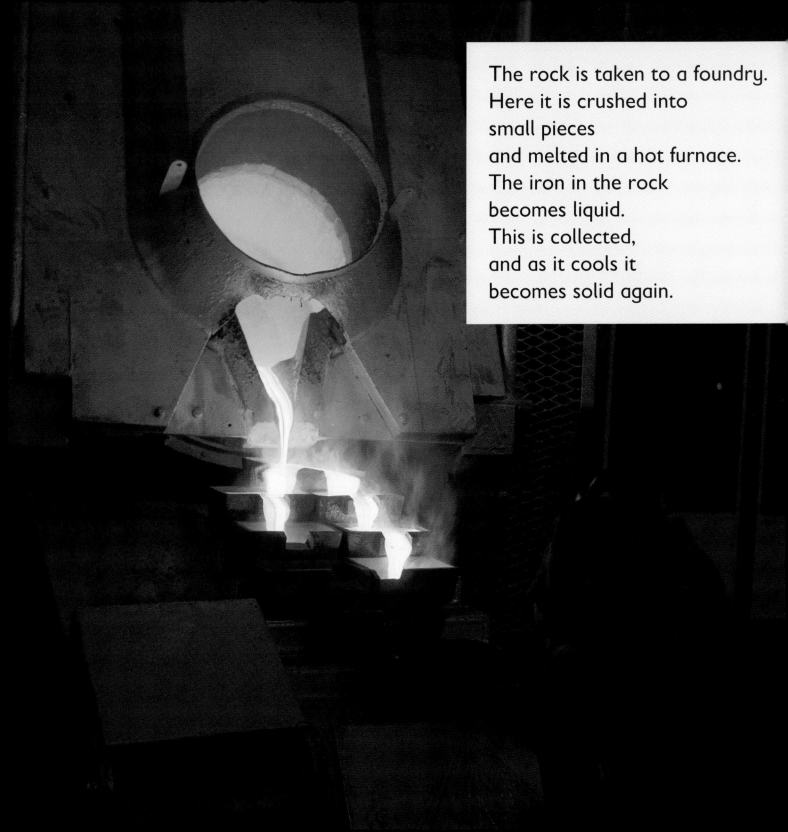

The rock is taken to a foundry.
Here it is crushed into
small pieces
and melted in a hot furnace.
The iron in the rock
becomes liquid.
This is collected,
and as it cools it
becomes solid again.

Most metals are obtained
by heating rock.
A few, like gold,
can be cut from the rock . . .

or collected as "dust" from streams which have washed over rocks containing a pure metal.

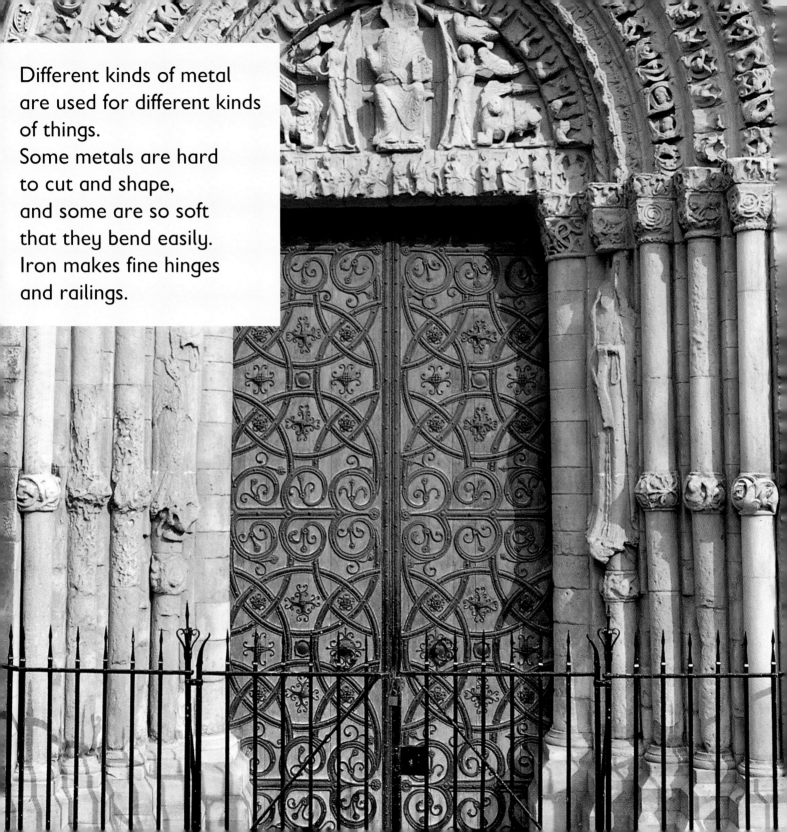

Different kinds of metal
are used for different kinds
of things.
Some metals are hard
to cut and shape,
and some are so soft
that they bend easily.
Iron makes fine hinges
and railings.

Soft metals,
like gold and silver,
are much more suitable
for making beautiful jewellery.

Long ago precious metals
were used by Kings
and Emperors
to show how powerful
they were.

Even the metal armour
they wore in battle
was richly decorated.

We use metals
to make all kinds of tools.
Some metals can be sharpened
to give a cutting edge.

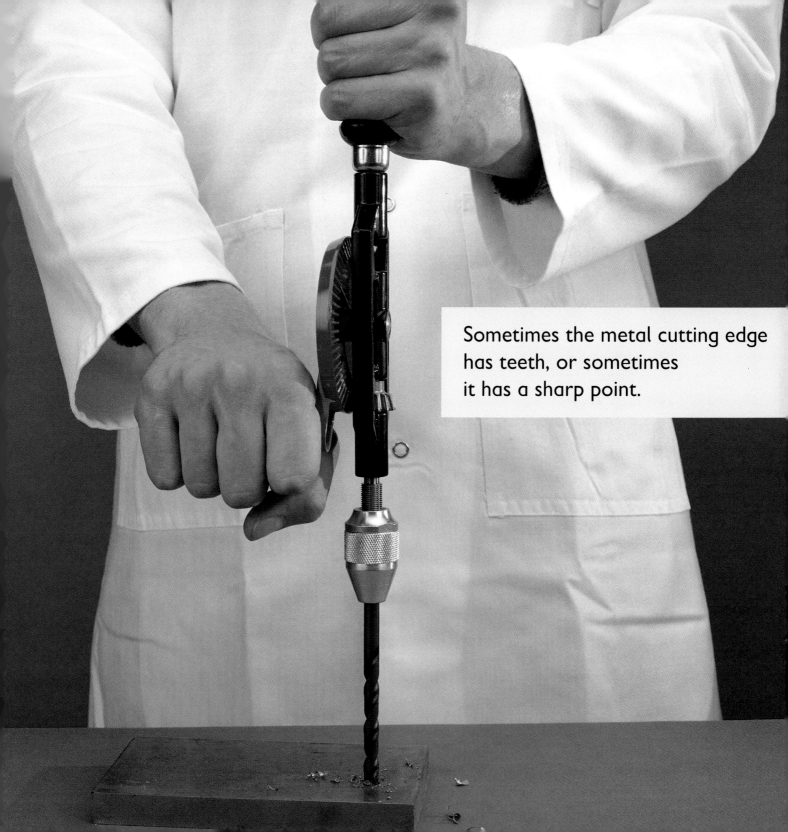

Sometimes the metal cutting edge has teeth, or sometimes it has a sharp point.

We use metal tools
to make metal machines –
to make ships, and the engines
which power them ...

to make trains and the track
along which they run . . .

to make farm machinery . . .

to make cars, buses
and bicycles,
and the signs
which their drivers follow.

We wear things
made of metal.
Belts, buckles and buttons,
zips and fastenings,
hooks and eyes . . .

and carry things made of metal in our pockets – coins, pens, keys and combs.

Metal allows heat
to travel through it easily.
It does not catch alight.
Why are saucepans made
of metal
and their handles
made of wood?

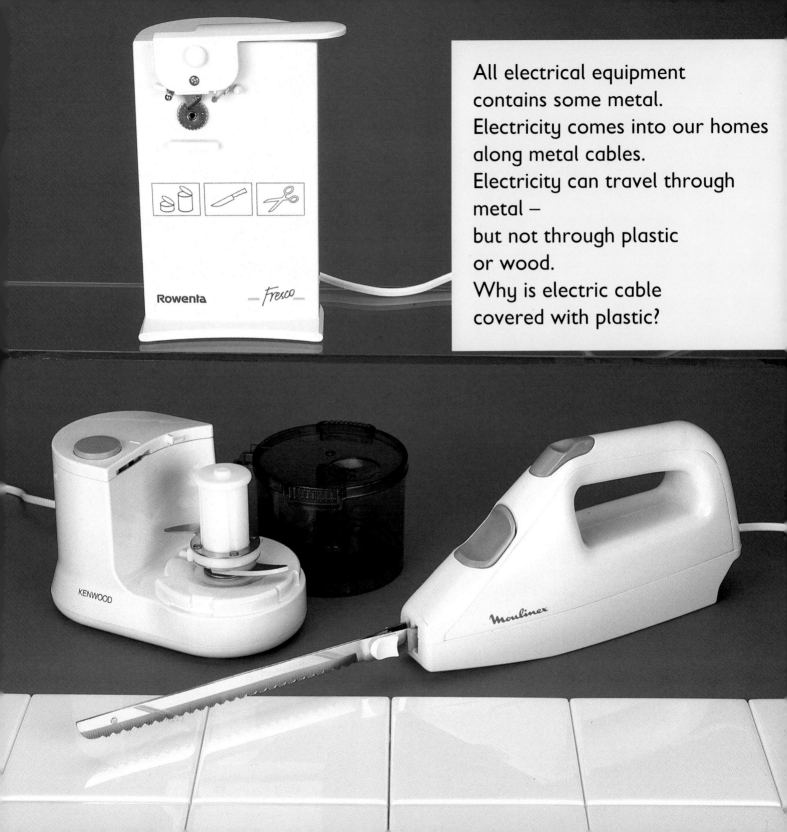

All electrical equipment contains some metal.
Electricity comes into our homes along metal cables.
Electricity can travel through metal –
but not through plastic or wood.
Why is electric cable covered with plastic?

We use metal
out of doors too!
In our towns and cities
there are statues
made from metal ...

and play equipment
made of metal
in our parks.

When different kinds of metal
are hot and liquid
they can be mixed together
to make a new metal.
This is called an alloy.
Brass is an alloy
of copper and zinc.
It is very tough and is often
used for making weights.

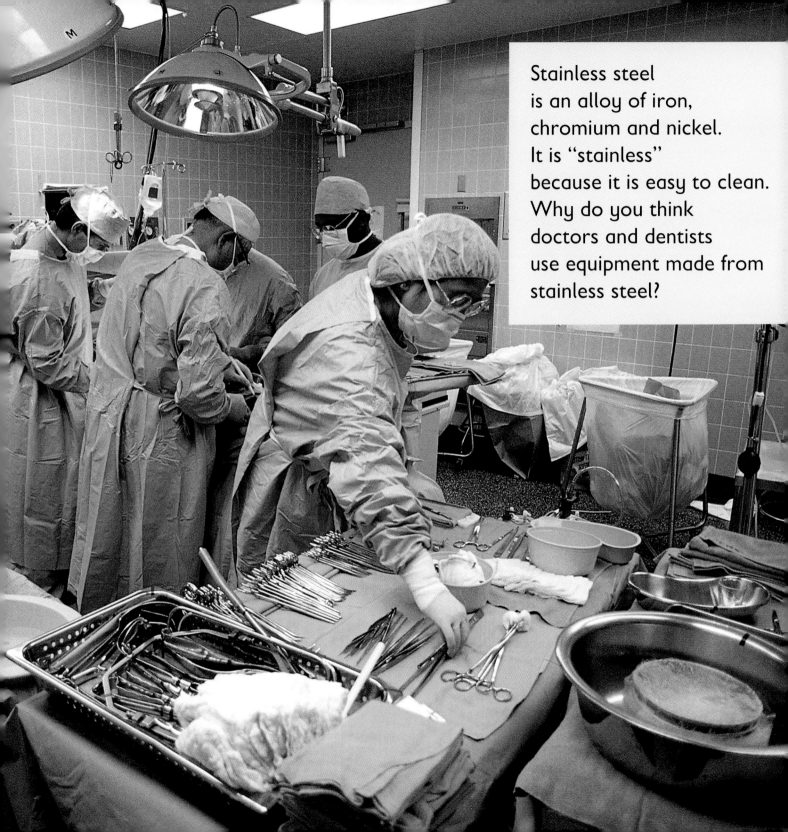

Stainless steel
is an alloy of iron,
chromium and nickel.
It is "stainless"
because it is easy to clean.
Why do you think
doctors and dentists
use equipment made from
stainless steel?

Some metal alloys are strong and light and can withstand hot and cold. These are used to build spaceships ...

to make the clothing
worn by the men and women
who travel in them –
and for the equipment
they use.

Even the equipment used by deep sea divers has metal in it.

Our world would be
a strange place
without metals.
It is odd to think
that metals are found
in rocks in the ground.

About this book

This book is designed for use in the home, kindergarten and infant school.

Parents can share the book with young children. Its aim is to bring into focus some of the elements of life and living which are all too often taken for granted. To develop fully, all young children need to have their understanding of the world deepened and the language they use to express their ideas extended. This book, and others in the series, takes the everyday things of the child's world and explores them, harnessing curiosity and wonder in a purposeful way.

For those working with young children each book is designed to be used both as a picture book, which explores ideas and concepts and as a starting point to talk and exploration. The pictures have been selected because they are of interest in themselves and also because they include elements which will promote enquiry. Talk can lead to displays of items and pictures collected by children and teacher. Pictures and collages can be made by the children themselves.

Everything in our environment is of interest to the growing child. The purpose of these books is to extend and develop that interest.

Henry Pluckrose